First Steps out of Eating Disorders

Dr Kate Middleton
and Dr Jane Smith

LION

WEST DUNBARTONSHIRE LIBRARIES	
C 03 0221457	
HJ	26-Aug-2010
616.852	£4.99
CL	

Copyright © 2010 Kate Middleton and
Jane Smith
This edition copyright © 2010 Lion Hudson
The authors assert the moral right
to be identified as the authors of this work

A Lion Book
an imprint of
Lion Hudson plc
Wilkinson House, Jordan Hill Road,
Oxford OX2 8DR, England
www.lionhudson.com
ISBN 978 0 7459 5520 9

Distributed by:
UK: Marston Book Services, PO Box 269,
Abingdon, Oxon, OX14 4YN
USA: Trafalgar Square Publishing, 814
N. Franklin Street, Chicago, IL 60610
USA Christian Market: Kregel Publications,
PO Box 2607, Grand Rapids, MI 49501
First edition 2010
10 9 8 7 6 5 4 3 2 1 0
All rights reserved

A catalogue record for this book is available
from the British Library

Typeset in 10/13 ITC Stone Serif
Printed and bound in Malta

Contents

Introduction

Eating is an essential part of life. It is something we all have to do regularly in order to give our bodies the nourishment they need. It's something that you might expect to be instinctive and problem-free. Unfortunately this is far from the case. Rates of eating disorders continue to rise – and every case of an eating disorder means that there is someone for whom eating has become a battleground, tangled up with their emotions and their life in such a way that they find it hard to think clearly any more. Many sufferers start out aiming to gain control, but end up in situations where they have to admit that they are not in control at all. For every sufferer there are also families, friends, and other people who care for them. An eating disorder is a battle that involves everyone around a sufferer.

Before we start, there are three things that need to be made clear:

First, this book is a guide to how to take the *first steps* out of an eating disorder. It is an introduction to a very complex area. We hope that it will help you to make sense of where you – or the person you are worried about – are, and how to start making some positive changes. But

eating disorders are difficult and devious problems. There are often many different elements or issues going on for someone who's suffering, and it's not possible to cover *everything* that might be relevant for you here. If you want to know more, do refer to the Useful resources section at the end for some suggestions for further reading, and sources of additional help and advice.

Secondly, please be aware that eating disorders can also have serious physical side effects. This book is not a substitute for seeking good expert help, and it is essential that anyone suffering with an eating disorder speaks to their doctor about it (you'll find some tips for how to approach your doctor in Chapter 6).

Finally, one of the cruellest effects of an eating disorder is to make you feel as if you are all alone. Sufferers often believe that no one understands how they are feeling, and carers – parents in particular – can feel blamed for the eating disorder and end up isolated and struggling with their own emotions as well as the eating disorder. We want you to know that you are not alone. Millions of people across the world have suffered from an eating disorder. Most importantly of all, millions have *recovered* from an eating disorder. There *is* life after an eating disorder. We hope that this book helps you to take the first steps towards the rest of your life.

1
About "eating disorders"

Before we look at how to work your way *out* of an eating disorder, we need to look at how the eating disorder *developed* in the first place. Think of an eating disorder as a bit like setting out on a road trip – and ending up somewhere you never wanted to be. It's difficult to work out how to get home without first understanding where you are now and how you got there.

So let's start by making sure that we actually understand that basic term "eating disorder". Definitions vary, but most specialists would agree that an eating disorder occurs when disordered eating patterns – whatever they are – start to have a serious impact on a person's emotional and/or physical health.

Emotional impact...
What we mean by this is that your eating and any issues to do with it *really* bother you. An eating disorder has a big impact on how you are feeling day to day. Sufferers

describe how simple things like the weight shown on the scales in the morning when they get up can have the power to destroy their day.

What people say...

The anticipation is there from the moment I wake up. I always weigh myself first thing, after I have got up and gone to the loo. Walking over to the scales I feel really nervous. I know that whatever happens next will define my day – whether I will feel good about myself, happy and confident, or be demoralized, depressed and find it hard to even get dressed and face work. I know my eating will be affected, whether it's that I set myself strict rules for the rest of the day and try to eat very little, or that I lose control and overeat. I know my relationships will be affected because my husband hates it when I get obsessed by my weight. And most of all I know, deep down, that my life is being ruined by this because every day has the potential to be ruined just by the numbers on that machine when I stand on it.
  Emma

Physical impact...

Whether it is under-eating or overeating, the chaotic patterns which eating disorders trigger are damaging to your health. There is no debating this. Some health effects are short term, others are long term, but the uncomfortable truth is that eating disorders can and do take people's lives.

What people say...

When she died we were utterly stunned. We knew that she had been having problems. A bit of overeating, a bit of under-eating – we thought it was just a phase. But it turns out it was much more. I wish there was some way we could go back in time and help her before it was too late. Because we're not even sure that she realized just how serious things were.

A parent

Mythbuster

Only women get eating disorders.
No! It's very important that we set the record straight on this one immediately. Although most experts agree that eating disorders are more common in women, there is also a clear trend for more and more men and boys to be struggling. Eating disorders can affect anyone – the young and the old, boys and girls, men and women.

There are three main eating disorders – defined in the next chapter – but it is important to remember that not everyone will receive a clear-cut diagnosis of one of these. Many people struggle with their eating, but never develop a problem serious enough to be diagnosed as a clinical eating disorder. Others have serious problems which affect their life and health, but may not fit into a clear category for one of the eating disorders or may swing between different eating disorders. Perhaps the largest numbers of sufferers, however, are those who never seek help. Shame, guilt or fear about what they are experiencing means that they never get diagnosed and instead suffer in silence. If this is you then take heart – you are not alone. Your eating problems do not mean that there is something wrong with you. They are simply a sign that you have become caught up in a vicious cycle which can be very hard to break out of.

The good news – recovery *is* possible!

The good news – and in fact the most important thing to remember from this chapter is – that it *is* possible to recover from all of these eating disorders! Eating disorders can bring with them overwhelming feelings of despair and hopelessness. Often people have tried to break out of them, but because they tend to repeat the same patterns again and again, they set themselves up to fail. Good support and specialist treatment can be hard to find, but really can transform people's lives. We'll talk much more about recovery and what it *really* is in Chapter 5.

Over to you

Throughout this book you will see there are opportunities for you to apply what has been said to your own situation. If you are struggling with an eating problem yourself, you may find it helpful to get a notebook or diary where you can write your responses to these sections, and work through the exercises suggested. For those who are concerned about someone else, don't just skip these sections. You should find them interesting, and also useful in helping you understand why your friend or loved one is struggling. You may also be able to work through these sections with them at a later date.

I think I might have an eating disorder...

If you yourself are struggling with what may or may not be an eating disorder, it can be very hard to admit to yourself just how bad things are. Realizing that the cycles you are caught in are actually not helping you, but making things worse, is very scary. Most people develop an eating disorder because they are desperately trying to hold things together, not to let people down, to keep going. To admit that this has gone badly wrong is not easy. So if this is you, well done for even reading this book. It will have taken a lot of courage, and we want you to know that we understand that. Try to give yourself time to read the whole book and think through what's inside. But do realize that this book is a starting point, not the whole solution. It will give you some of the tools you need to get started on working towards recovery, but you will need good support from family and friends who care for you, and often from professionals too. Don't try to do this on your own – you will need some help. You deserve to live life to the full – not restricted by the prison of an eating disorder.

I am really worried about someone else

Trying to support someone else as they work towards recovery from an eating disorder can be really hard. Chapter 7 in particular looks at the many challenges of caring for someone else, and at what you can do to really make a difference and help someone break out of their eating disorder. As for the rest of the book, you may find that some sections are written from a sufferer's perspective. Do read these sections – they will help you to discover the kind of thinking processes that your loved one is experiencing and you can help them to understand these and work towards recovery. You might be able to use some of the exercises, questions or sections with the person you are caring for. Do also check out the suggestions for getting more support. Many carers say that it is not they who need support but the sufferer. But the more support *you* get, and the more you understand,

the more expert your support will be – and that is good
for everyone.

You have to be skinny to have an eating disorder.
This is a really important misconception. Many people,
including some sufferers, get caught in the mistaken belief
that to be taken seriously, or to be diagnosed and given
help, they have to be skinny. You can be suffering with an
eating disorder at *any* weight, and even when weight loss
does occur it may not be obvious.

2
The road to an eating disorder

Whether you are reading this book for yourself, or for someone else, the chances are that you are experiencing behaviour around food which seems pretty illogical. At the same time, even if you are not a sufferer, most people admit that eating disorders may feel uncomfortably familiar. Anyone who has ever felt bad about a bit of weight gain, gone on a diet or overeaten after a loss of control or willpower understands some of the feelings involved. But for those caught up in an eating disorder it has become something altogether more powerful and more difficult to escape from.

There are hundreds of theories about why and how people develop eating disorders. Here is an "in a nutshell" summary of the road to an eating disorder. Remember everyone is different – but the chances are you will recognize some of these stages:

Stage 1: Chasing the illusion – if only I were thinner...

An eating disorder begins when someone who is struggling with other things in their life starts to look to controlling their weight in order to try to sort things out. Our society constantly feeds us the message that being thin equals being successful. For some people – when life has dealt them some serious blows or when they find it hard to like anything about themselves or their circumstances – the lure of this apparent "cure-all" solution is irresistible.

"If only I were thinner," they think, "things would be different and I would feel better." For some people this isn't a conscious decision, but more a sense of becoming overwhelmed with an inner "need" to lose weight, perhaps seeing fat as evidence of "bad" in them and something they need to change by losing weight. Still others may have lost weight as a result of something else – illness or other emotional problems – and suddenly find that they have developed a fear of gaining weight – and the desire to lose more.

And this is the lie that is at the root of most eating disorders. Whatever the tough stuff in their life that people are trying to escape or change, they fix on their eating and weight because it offers something that they *can* or *should* be able to change – and which they believe will make them happier. Their weight becomes the scapegoat – in their mind it is the cause of all that is wrong with their life.

Stage 2: Setting limits

The next step in developing an eating disorder is to resolve to restrict their eating. They set limits or restrictions on what they do and do not eat, following diet plans or making a list of "bad" foods to be avoided at all costs. Some aim to eat as little as possible, counting calories or fat grams or perhaps going on a "detox". Strict rules are set – and they have every intention of following them precisely – because this is what they have pinned their hopes on to make everything better.

Stage 3: Success or failure?

Some people find – perhaps due to some features of their personality or more practical things such as whether they can avoid eating family meals or food planned and cooked by someone else – that they are successful at controlling what they eat. They lose weight, perhaps quite fast. This immediate feedback is powerful. It shows that they are getting somewhere, and it motivates them to keep going. But in spite of this success, they still feel just as bad. So they persist with their plan – perhaps even stepping up the control and taking more things out of their diet. Some may have moments when they do eat – or even when they lose control and overeat – but overall they keep up the strict dieting. Weight loss continues, and their resolve never drops.

This is the slippery slide into **anorexia nervosa**. Here the drive to keep on losing weight becomes so powerful that even the bodily warning signs are ignored, signs that the body is struggling to exist at such a low weight. Anorexia causes someone to be single-minded and utterly determined. Sufferers often become so convinced that losing weight is the solution that they feel they are fat even when the reality is that they are dangerously thin. They may resort to over-exercise and may make themselves sick as well in order to lose as much weight as possible, and as a result may become at risk of serious physical problems.

A second group of people try just as hard, but cannot sustain their restrictive eating pattern, whether for practical reasons or as a result of their personality. Their body, which has been existing on a much reduced diet, craves food. Control breaks down and they eat – often the very foods that they had planned to avoid, and sometimes in large quantities. This leads to the start of binge eating – periods of time when they feel they lose control and eat much more than would be considered "normal" in those circumstances. As binges develop they tend to get worse, and the guilt that goes alongside them is horrendous. Most people end a binge overwhelmed with self-hatred, frustration, and regret. They resolve never ever to let this happen again, and return to stage two, perhaps with a different diet or new (stricter) limits. Unfortunately they repeat the same mistakes and the whole cycle repeats itself again and again.

This cycle of restricting eating, then losing control and bingeing, is **binge eating disorder**. Binges happen several times a week, often on "forbidden" or high-calorie foods. As a result, sufferers are usually overweight or obese and often struggle dreadfully with the emotional impact of their weight. Many would say that they hate themselves, or their bodies, and that their eating is part of this painful cycle of self-hatred. Eating is powerfully linked with emotions and with other issues such as depression and loneliness. Sufferers feel helpless and hopeless and have usually tried diet after diet in an attempt to lose weight, only to regain it again.

The last group of sufferers also get caught in the restricting and bingeing cycle. Utterly frustrated by their inability to keep up the control required to meet their goals of weight loss, they often describe themselves as "failed anorexics" and despise their own inability to "succeed" at losing weight. For them, the emotions after a binge are so powerful that one day these feelings drive them to try to do something – anything – in order to stop the food they have eaten from leading to their gaining weight. They are overwhelmed by powerful negative emotions like guilt, shame, horror, self-hatred, and, most of all, a desire to turn the clock back and not to have done what they just did. They begin purging – something they believe removes the food from their body without it being absorbed, or counteracts the extra calories they have eaten.

This is how **bulimia nervosa** develops. Sufferers may try to make themselves sick or take laxatives, believing that they speed up the passage of food through the body. Others exercise compulsively every day to try to counteract the extra calories or they take diet pills. Whatever they do, this "purging" becomes part of the cycle – the dieting and restricting, then the losing control and bingeing, then the purging and trying to restore control.

The cycle repeats itself over and over, and each time it starts again sufferers try desperately to change. But as they restrict their eating and deny themselves foods, they set the cycle up again. Eventually control breaks down and the bingeing starts once more, with the risk of triggering serious physical complications. Sufferers struggle with shame about what they are doing and can hide it very well. As a result bulimia can continue unnoticed for years.

3

Eating disorders – the dark side

Eating disorders do not happen overnight. They are not just about people going on diets for the sake of vanity or fashion. At first they feel like the solution, but in fact they cause many more problems than they solve. Eating disorders are very devious and keep you thinking very short term – a bit like driving a car without looking at a map. The longer-term impact that they can have on your body and on your life often creeps up on you. Many sufferers read accounts of other people struggling with their health or well-being and think, "That will never happen to me." However, the risk is that if you are travelling somewhere without planning where you are going, you might end up somewhere you never wanted to be.

It may be that you are surrounded by other people who are pushing you to "do something about your eating" or nagging you to go to the doctor. One of them may even have bought you this book! Most sufferers find it hard to accept the worries other people have about them. This chapter is not an attempt to nag you or to try to persuade you of anything. But it is vitally important that you are aware of the truth about any risks you might be facing – and that you are therefore able to decide what you want to do next.

Over to you: How does your eating affect you?

Having read through the descriptions of the different eating disorders in Chapter 2, it's time to think about what is going on for you. Are there any things you noticed in the descriptions which relate to you? Note them down in a diary or notebook. This needs to be a private record of what is going on in your life, and your thoughts, behaviour, and feelings – so do be honest with yourself. Whatever you decide to do (or not do) about your eating problems, it's important that you give yourself the chance to be realistic about what is going on. Ask yourself the following questions:

- What do you feel right now about your weight? Does this match what other people think or do they have different opinions?
- Now consider how your eating and/or your weight affects your everyday life. Does your eating or your weight compromise your choices? Does it result in other consequences that you might wish to avoid?
- Now to think to the future – what would you love to do with your life? Do you have any big dreams, ambitions or plans? It doesn't matter if these are things you want to do next year or in decades to come – write them down!

Effects on your health

First of all we need to look at the subject no one wants to think about: the possible impact eating disorders can have on your health. Physical problems are a bit like the side effects of an eating disorder – not something you ever intended to happen, but very real. At first you might feel fine, but as time goes on you are likely to notice the strain that the eating disorder puts on your body. Here's a summary of some of the common health risks associated with eating disorders:

Common health risks of...
...losing too much weight:

Side effect	You might notice this because...
Low blood pressure	You feel (or even do) faint if you stand up too fast. Your circulation will get worse too, so cold hands and feet are another sign.
Weakening of your heart	When your body runs out of fat to use for energy it uses up muscle – including your heart muscle – and a slower pulse occurs as the heart conserves energy. A normal pulse is around 80–90 beats per minute. You may experience chest pains, heart problems, and ultimately even heart attacks.
Other muscles being weakened	You might feel weaker or not have as much stamina as before.
Anaemia (not enough red blood cells in your blood)	This also affects how well you can be active – you might notice you get out of breath more easily (red blood cells carry the oxygen to your muscles, so with too few you have to breathe faster to help get more oxygen moved around) and feel tired or sluggish.

Infertility	This affects women in particular because if you lose too much weight or lose weight too quickly, your periods might become irregular or stop altogether (they usually start again when your weight and eating improve, but some women do see long-term problems).
Osteoporosis	This is a tricky one as you probably won't notice anything at first. Osteoporosis causes your bones to be weak and brittle. Not eating properly during adolescence means your bones aren't strengthened as much as they should be, so when you lose bone strength (as we all do when we get older), your bones can become too weak. You can also lose bone strength much more quickly if your periods stop for too long.
Other side effects	If your weight is too low you will feel the cold a lot more than other people. This can be really horrid and some people struggle to ever get warm – even in the height of summer. You might notice circulation problems with your hands or feet as well.
	A fine hair called lanugo can grow over the body.
	Problems with sleeping mean that you feel tired, listless, and exhausted.
	You will probably feel depressed and emotional.
	Bones really are not designed to be sat on and if you lose the fat covering them, you will find hard surfaces really uncomfortable. Sitting on hard chairs or even taking a bath can become, literally, a real pain.

...purging:

Side effect	You might notice this because...
Loss of electrolytes	This is the most serious side effect. If you make yourself sick or take too many laxatives, you lose a lot of water – and dissolved in that water are vital chemicals called electrolytes. The balance of these chemicals in your body is essential for, among other things, keeping your heart beating regularly, as well as for the normal function of your brain. At first there are no signs of levels being too low, but if you keep on losing electrolytes or if levels of some key ones get too low, you might experience symptoms as serious as heart failure or fits.
Digestive problems	Purging completely interrupts the normal processes involved in your digestive system. Making yourself sick can weaken the natural valve at the top of your stomach, meaning that acid leaks up causing heartburn and indigestion. Taking too many laxatives upsets the natural rhythm of the bowel, causing problems like constipation or diarrhoea. Over time these problems can get more serious so that people struggle to keep food down at all or get more serious problems like irritable bowel syndrome or food intolerances.

| "Emergency" side effects | Self-induced vomiting can lead to rupturing the stomach, and there are also many reports of people choking on things they were using to make themselves sick. Abusing laxatives can also cause serious problems – mainly through the loss of electrolytes (see above), but also due to the effect on the digestive system. |

...gaining too much weight:

Side effect	You might notice this because...
Cardiovascular disease	This is a long-term side effect – eating too much unhealthy food over the years causes changes to the blood vessels in your body. Fatty deposits build up and can start to block the vessels. You might not notice symptoms for years, but it can lead to serious problems like angina, strokes, and ultimately heart attacks.
Metabolic problems including type two diabetes	This is caused by eating too many sugary foods over a long period of time. Diabetes can cause serious health problems and is linked with heart disease. Again you might not notice many symptoms – this form of diabetes is usually picked up in tests by your doctor.
Mobility problems	The heavier you are the greater the strain on your joints. Joint problems like arthritis can be linked to being overweight, as can a whole host of joint aches and pains. Once these are a problem they can make it even more difficult to start exercising and losing weight.

| Increased risk of other health problems | Being overweight and eating an unhealthy diet is linked with an increased risk of all kinds of health problems including many cancers. The good news is that improving your diet and losing weight really does make a difference – but it's really important to remember the long-term risks of what you are doing. |

Over to you: Your health

Have you noticed any changes to your health since you have been struggling with the eating disorder? Have you experienced any of the side effects in the lists above? Are there any health problems that anyone else is worried about for you – for example, your doctor or relatives? (Please note: some of these physical effects are *really* serious. That's why it is so important you see a doctor and get your physical health checked out. If you are noticing symptoms, do not delay – arrange an appointment! For more on this, see Chapter 6.)

Eating disorders can affect a lot more than just your health. They can have a major impact on friendships, relationships, your social life, and even your work or studies. Many people find that they have to stop doing things which they used to enjoy or which they wanted to be able to do in order to achieve another goal – such as getting good grades in order to study for a particular job or profession. Meanwhile, of course, no man (or woman!) is an island – all sufferers have to deal with the reactions of other people to what is going on. Even if you do not think that your eating disorder is a problem, other people might do – and not all will respond positively.

Over to you: Other downsides...

Are there other things in your life which your eating disorder has affected? Can you think of anything which you are no longer able to do, or which you avoid doing, because it is related to eating or to other issues linked to your eating disorder? How has your eating disorder changed your relationships with other people? And, finally, has it had any impact on your work or studies? How might this affect things for you in the future?

It is really important that you are able to take a realistic look at the negative aspects of your eating disorder. This is to make sure that you do not accidentally take a path which leads you somewhere you do not intend to go. So far we've only considered how your eating disorder is affecting you *now*. But an eating disorder is not a short-term strategy – untreated eating disorders can last a lifetime. You need to think about what the negative impacts of your eating might be if it continued the way it is now. Would your health worsen and would you notice other negative consequences?

Over to you: Short- and long-term "cons" of an eating disorder

One way to make sure you are taking a realistic look at the negative aspects of your eating disorder is to write them down. Make a list of the "cons" affecting you right now. Try to include everything, so think about what you wrote down in response to the last two "over to you" boxes in this chapter. Now write another list, this time thinking about what the cons would be at a time in the future *assuming that your eating disorder carried on the way it is now*. You might want to choose a key time such as your next birthday or a significant date, like when you are due to start or finish college. What would the cons be then – what impact might your eating disorder have had by this point in the future?

This chapter has been about helping you to take a realistic look at how your eating disorder might affect you in a negative way. Hopefully the chapter has helped you to think about where you are right now – and where you are headed. The decision to work towards recovery is a personal one and one only you can make. Give yourself some time to ponder these things. If you know your eating disorder will eventually start to cause you problems or stop you from achieving the things you dream of, at some stage you need to let it go. But before you can make that decision, it's just as important to be aware of what your eating disorder *gives* you – and that is what the next chapter is about.

Over to you: One last question

Before moving on from this chapter, go back to the section above where you wrote down your life ambitions, dreams, and plans. How might they be affected if you continue with your eating disorder? Might it affect the chances of their coming true?

4

Why do people develop eating disorders?

Eating disorders are like any good salesman selling dodgy merchandise. They do not tell you about the negative side until you are hooked in. People develop eating disorders because they find at first that they produce some kind of positive effect. So enough of the negative – let's look now at what you feel your eating disorder *gives* you. It is really important to understand this, as it is part of recovery. You need to know why you developed an eating disorder in the first place, and what need it was meeting for you, so that you can learn more positive ways to meet that need instead and find real freedom!

"Causes" of eating disorders

Many things have been linked with an increased risk of developing an eating disorder. Here are just some of the common experiences that can be linked to struggles with your eating and weight:

- Bullying
- Abuse
- Problems with low self-esteem
- Traumatic experiences such as violent or sexual assault
- Anxiety
- Depression
- Stress
- Pressure (from yourself or others) to achieve
- Living or working in an environment where there is pressure to be thin (for example, dancing or gymnastics)
- Previous problems with weight (often in childhood)

Offering hope

One way eating disorders can help people is by offering something that they cannot achieve elsewhere. This may be a feeling of being in control or of achievement which cannot be found in other areas. Other people find that their eating disorder helps them to communicate something about themselves which they feel unable to explain in another way. Or it presents a practical solution to something, perhaps offering a way out of commitments or pressures, or making sure that their and other people's expectations are lowered.

Changing the apparently unchangeable

Of course another way an eating disorder can help is by changing something which otherwise seems impossible to change. Some people find that they feel more confident – or hope to gain confidence once they lose weight. Others are looking for a way to feel less anxious, or become better at friendships or relationships.

Helping you cope

Finally, an eating disorder usually develops as part of an attempt to deal with difficult and painful emotions that are linked to situations going on around you. It may be that you have been through an experience which has been particularly traumatic and challenged your view of yourself. Situations you faced when you were growing up may have left you with some difficult beliefs about yourself or about what other people think of you. Or you may be coping with something which is ongoing and very difficult to deal with. Some people find that life is simply throwing too much at them, and their eating disorder develops as part of their desperate attempt to cope.

Over to you: How does it tie in with the rest of your life?

Can you think of anything your eating disorder offers you that you cannot find elsewhere in your life? It may be one of the things suggested – or something else. Are there any aspects of your life which have changed in a positive way since you developed the eating disorder? What about how you experience the world around you? Are there any areas that you hope your eating disorder will change? Are there any differences that you have already noticed?

Finally, are you aware of issues in your life that you find difficult to deal

with or cope with? It may be that other people link your eating disorder to something you have been through. Are there any areas of your life that you feel may be linked to your eating disorder?

Desperately seeking a solution

One of the reasons eating disorders are so dangerous is because at first they really do feel like a solution rather than a problem.

What people say…

All my life I had been invisible, ineffective and irrelevant. I had no confidence and my life was falling apart. Then when I went on that first diet, things seemed to change. I lost some weight and people really noticed. They'd comment on it – which made me feel really good. It boosted my confidence and I felt more able to go out and socialize. I felt like finally I had found something I was really good at. People admired me and that felt really good. Plus it felt like I was finally on the move – things were changing, and at that stage I thought it was for the better.

    Jack

The problem is that the positive things an eating disorder provides really don't last. Although trying to control your eating might help in the short term, it doesn't help you with things that are *really* making you deeply unhappy. Imagine that you are in a dark room. The darkness is rather like the unhappiness you are experiencing. What you really need to do is to find a way of getting rid of that darkness for ever. An eating disorder doesn't do that – instead it's similar to lighting a candle. It may well make things feel better for a while, but it doesn't deal with the underlying problem. Worst of all, it's only a temporary solution – candles burn out, and in the same way an eating disorder takes its toll on your body and sooner or later will start to cause you problems. You risk pushing your body to the limit, burning your candle right down to the stage where there is a real chance of serious physical health problems as a result.

As much as it is important to understand what an eating disorder provides, it is also essential to be aware of how this changes over time – especially whether it is really worth it in the long term. Remember, an eating disorder causes many more problems than it solves. You need to think about the pros of your eating disorder *alongside the cons* you noted in the previous chapter. Most people find that over time – particularly as the number of cons tends to increase – an eating disorder simply is not worth it. That is why it is so important to think about recovery and what that might mean for you.

Over to you: Pros and cons

In the last chapter we looked at the cons of an eating disorder both in the short term (i.e. now) and in the long term. If you think about the pros of your eating disorder – the points discussed in this chapter – how do you see them changing as time goes on? If your eating disorder continues, will the pros change?

You might want to combine the pros with the cons you wrote down in the last chapter. Try writing two lists – one with the pros and cons of your eating disorder now and another looking at the pros and cons at some time in the future. You can put them in two tables so that you can compare them. Here's an example from a girl called Jenny. She was struggling with anorexia and finding it really hard to think about leaving it behind. Here are her pros and cons…

NOW

PROS	CONS
Feel more confident.	Feel tired all the time.
Helps me feel in control.	Am always cold.
People notice me.	Periods have stopped and I am scared of ending up unable to have children.
Means I don't go to school.	
People expect less of me.	Parents are always on at me.
Feel better about myself when I have lost weight.	Struggle with depression – feel really awful sometimes.
People look up to me because of my self-control.	Cannot go out with friends.

IN FIVE YEARS' TIME

PROS	CONS
Will still be thin.	Health will probably be really bad. Will still not be able to have kids and might want to by then.
Will still feel in control.	
People will still expect less of me.	Will be on my own – all my friends will have gone off to college and will get jobs, but I will still not be able to.
	Will be stuck with parents – they probably won't let me get a flat while I am still ill.
	I will still be having times of feeling really terrible. Will I be able to cope with these? Not sure it is worth it.

PROS	CONS
	I will have missed out on going to college so I won't be able to do the job I want to. Not sure what my life will be about.
	Would like to get married really but this is unlikely while I am still ill and stuck inside the house.
	Don't want to be known as "the anorexic one".
	Will probably have lost touch with old friends who might get fed up of me being so miserable.

Over to you

What are *your* pros and cons? When you have completed your own chart, have a serious think about it. You might find it helpful to talk it over with someone else. What impact will your eating disorder have on you in the long term? Are there changes you need to make or things you want to avoid happening?

5

All about recovery – where do you want to get to?

As you have probably gathered, in this book "recovery" is a word you will hear a lot – it is our main focus. However, recovery is very rarely clearly defined – and that is a shame because it can mean different things to different people. If you are in the midst of an eating disorder and trying to decide whether to let it go and start working towards "recovery", you need to know what *real* recovery is all about – so you can decide if it is something you want, and also so you know when you have got there!

Preparing for recovery – some top tips!

1 Know that it is achievable.

2 Realize that the eating disorder may appear to be the solution, but actually is also the problem you need to get rid of.

3 Find out and understand what recovery is and is not.

4 Set realistic aims for recovery – think of it as a journey and a process, one that has forward steps, but also some backward ones at times. Just concentrating on a healthy weight or stopping purging is not the whole focus of recovery.

5 Look at your motivation for recovery. Why do you want to overcome your eating disorder?

6 Set realistic targets and goals for yourself. Don't try to do it all in one step!

7 Don't let setbacks get you down. They are part of the recovery process. In fact many recovered sufferers admit they learned from setbacks, so prepare for them and use them towards recovery.

Defining recovery?

What people say...

Coming home from the clinic where I'd had to gain weight back to my normal weight for height and age was one of the hardest times of my life and hardly anyone recognized that. I looked just the same as everyone else my age. I no longer looked anorexic, but I still felt anorexic, just in a bigger body which I didn't want to be in. Thankfully the therapy and support I had received and continued to receive helped me see my life and myself differently, but it was very hard to begin with and my recovery grew slowly with time and with a lot of support and encouragement from my family and from the professionals helping me.

Amy, recovering from anorexia

The usual definition of recovery focuses on "being back to normal". Of course for many people with an eating disorder this brings to mind thoughts of having to go back to how they felt before – distressed and unhappy – but now having "lost" the option of controlling their weight. You can therefore understand why to many the concept of "recovery" is a difficult one. "Back to normal" also risks placing too much focus on visible aspects such as eating and weight, meaning that recovery might be measured by looking at these things rather than by how people are *actually feeling*. Particularly after a spell in hospital to improve their physical health, some sufferers find that people assume they are recovered, when in fact the mental and emotional turmoil inside has not yet been treated.

Over to you: What do you think recovery is?

When you think of the word "recovery", what does it mean to you? Can you write a sentence or two about what you think real recovery is? You might also want to add a note about anything that you feel really *isn't* part of recovery as well.

Of course, real recovery is about much more than just weight gain or stabilization, or even just stopping bingeing or purging (although these issues may have to be urgently addressed before any other support or therapy can be offered if they are causing serious physical harm). Recovery is a process; one that addresses the reasons why you are using food as a coping mechanism, together with how you see yourself and your life. Recovery is about learning to view things differently, being helped to find strategies that work for you, some of which will be to do with food and eating, others of which will be about your emotional responses to life and which involve your thinking and feelings. Real recovery takes time, and the support you get as you learn how to live differently after "official" treatment has finished is just as important.

What people say...

I think recovery is about being free; it's about being able to live my life normally without the restrictions, fears, and obsessions that dominated my day and all my thinking when I was ill. I have a full life now with so many new things in it that I know I wouldn't have if I was still ill – friends, a social life, hobbies and a career. I can go out with my friends and eat without worrying – I don't even think about it any more, whereas in the past I would have fretted beforehand and probably gone without food so I could justify going out. I would have made an excuse to eat little, would have scanned everything on the menu for the lowest fat and calories and would have felt miserable, guilty and just not part of it. I probably would have made an excuse and not gone in the first place or if I had I would have purged afterwards. I look back at those days and feel sorry for myself and for the wasted years but I also feel proud that I made it through and that all the hard work of recovery was worth it. I got my life back and more – a full life and a happy one.

Robin, recovered from bulimia

What is and isn't recovery?

We asked a group of recovered and recovering sufferers to list the things that were and were not part of real recovery. Have a read of their lists. Do you agree? Is there anything you would add?

RECOVERY IS:

✓ Freedom – from shame, guilt, obsessive thoughts, and from the need to achieve.

✓ Confidence and not being alone.

✓ Eating and food are no longer an issue.

✓ Balance – sometimes eating too much, sometimes too little, but not thrown back into an eating disorder.

✓ Being different.

✓ Letting go and finding a new identity.

✓ Being able to enjoy food.

✓ Having a wider perspective and more opportunity.

✓ Having a family.

✓ Building up self-esteem, self-acceptance, and dignity.

✓ Being able to eat "nice" foods without fear of losing control.

✓ Not being fearful.

✓ Being able to see yourself as you really are.

✓ Having more fun.

✓ Looking to the future and moving on.

- ✓ Accepting yourself and not being too hard on yourself.
- ✓ Relief and peace of mind.
- ✓ Accepting change and the things you cannot change.
- ✓ Letting go of the past.
- ✓ Having new thoughts – not staying trapped or static.
- ✓ Being able to give enough to yourself and as a result the best of yourself to others.
- ✓ Being honest and true to yourself and others.
- ✓ Handing over the uncontrollable to your higher power.
- ✓ Doing the right things and being selfless.
- ✓ Not taking it out on yourself when things go wrong, and being able to make some mistakes.
- ✓ Feeling you deserve recovery.

RECOVERY IS NOT:

- x Diets all the time.
- x Being chained to something else.
- x Just gaining weight.
- x Papering over the cracks.
- x Constant denial.
- x Magic wand (it isn't instant relief).
- x Never having any problems ever again (it's about dealing with them in a more positive way).

- x Just pleasing others.

- x Isolation.

- x Dishonesty.

- x Living in the past.

- x Dwelling on the past.

- x Ignoring your "inner self".

- x Revisiting previous habits.

- x Living a lie.

- x Harbouring bitterness.

- x Turning anger in on youself.

- x Guilt.

- x Starvation.

- x Depending too much on others.

- x Losing responsibility or control.

- x A never-ending cycle of activity.

- x Trying to achieve perfection.

Preparing for recovery – overcoming negative views of recovery

Remember that complete recovery from an eating disorder *is* possible! Sometimes people feel so hopeless that they don't begin to attempt or even consider recovery. Negative views from misinformed people don't help either – too many people have heard things said like "Once an anorexic always an anorexic" or "You're stuck with bulimia for life". Even some clinicians can paint a poor picture of recovery, with a negative outlook and low expectations, which does not encourage recovery. Some sufferers decide themselves, or are encouraged by others, to accept a version of recovery where they are able to "manage" their eating disorder, staying reasonably healthy and making sure their eating is mostly in control. However, this is not real recovery and often condemns them to a lifetime of the mental torture which underlies an eating disorder. You *can* be truly free! But you need to be sure why you want to work towards recovery and what, for you, this will really be.

What people say...

I think for me the further I get from the days where I was really ill with my eating disorder, the more I understand about real recovery. At first I thought I would never be able to eat without thinking about the calories or worrying about whether I had exercised enough to burn it off. Then years later I realized I was doing just that! I thought I would never be able to weigh myself, and banned scales from the house. I still don't weigh myself regularly now, but we do have scales and when I use them to weigh suitcases, etc., I can do that without it triggering any of the old feelings. Every stage I thought I would never pass, over time I have. I've now been recovered for over fifteen years and I know I will never slip back into that again. Even when a slight urge comes over me again, it doesn't tempt me for a minute. Why would I want to return to that? Any positives it gave me were definitely not worth it. My eating disorder was gradually taking everything from me – my friends, my family, my career, the things I enjoyed... recovery has given me everything – happiness, confidence, marriage, kids – all the things I never dared dream of. There's no contest!

Alex, recovered from anorexia

6
Finding help

Wherever you are in your journey towards recovery, getting help and support is vital. Recovery involves all kinds of different people – friends who can care for you and listen through the tough times, therapists who can help you to understand the emotional roots of the eating disorder, and physical and medical support for any health problems you are experiencing. Finding support is also an essential part of combating the main thing sufferers struggle with when working towards recovery – and that is loneliness. Eating disorders force you to keep a large part of your life secret, and people often become very isolated.

What people say...
When I look back, my every day consisted of how I could successfully avoid food and other people, especially anyone trying to interfere and threaten my eating disorder. Of course I shunned food but I also shunned everybody else and all their

enquiries or offers of help. I lived a lonely and volatile double life and hated myself for it.

Fiona, now recovered from bulimia

The first step – talking to your doctor...

As well as checking your physical health, this is the first step in getting help from a variety of other professionals. We know that your main concern will be how you feel emotionally, not physically – but you need to know that your health is good enough to give you time to work through the emotional issues behind your eating disorder, and that you are not at serious risk of any of the complications listed in Chapter 3. Too many people think they are fine, but then experience a sudden collapse, or another complication of their eating disorder, and have to be rushed into hospital for treatment for this physical problem. This can be really traumatic, and it can feel as if all your control has been taken from you. Getting your health checked out is an important part of staying in control.

Now we know that approaching your doctor may be an incredibly daunting prospect, so think about how you are going to do this. It's good to have some idea of what you want to say and how you will begin the conversation before you go, and going with a friend or family member may make it easier, you can run your words by them in advance. Another suggestion some people find helpful is writing a letter to your doctor and sending it a week or so before your visit. That means you can choose what you want to say carefully in the privacy of your own home, outlining the problems you are having, asking any questions in advance and mentioning anything you do not want them to do or say on the first visit. You might be able to say things you know you'd never get out when face to face. It also gives your doctor some warning that you are not just coming in with a cold or sore throat! They might be able to book a longer appointment to give you more time to chat, or suggest that you come in at a quieter time of day.

If you are unsure of who to approach within the surgery, then have a think about the doctors you know there and who you would feel more relaxed talking to. You could also chat to the practice nurse or ask the receptionists if any of the doctors have a particular interest in emotional health. You might be able to ask someone else (a friend or family member) to talk to the doctor or to the receptionists on your behalf. Alternatively you could see the doctor about another medical matter and get a feel for their manner. Whatever way, you are then prepared and can make some choices.

Over to you: Going to the doctor

If you have not already told your doctor about your eating disorder, you need to decide how and when you are going to do this. Write your ideas down in a notebook or diary. Include details such as when and how you plan to tell your doctor (jot down the appointment time and any notes about how you are going to tell him/her) and anything you are going to do to try to make it a bit easier (for example, writing a letter beforehand or taking a friend with you).

Your doctor's role

Your family doctor plays a really important role in your treatment. Their job is basically to be on your side and

to fight your corner and make sure that you get the help you need. Here are just some of the things that they might do for you:

- Perform an initial assessment of your eating problems.
- Provide medical checks and ongoing medical monitoring of your health (blood tests, weight checks, blood pressure).
- Coordinate other services to help you.
- Write referral letters and arrange appointments.

The first thing they should do is listen to you. In fact whatever else is going on, you should always feel supported by your doctor. They might not actually weigh you on your first visit – something which might come as a huge relief to you. If they do ask to weigh you and you would rather not be weighed, you can refuse, but do remember that knowing your weight is an important part of assessing any possible risk you might be facing. You can always ask not to see your weight yourself, or that the doctor does not say it out loud. The doctor might also want to do some other tests to rule out any physical reasons for weight loss or unusual eating habits.

Where else can I get help?

In addition to your doctor, there are a whole host of other people and services around to support you as you work towards recovery. Here are just some of them – with some notes about what they do, and what to expect if you come across them:

Eating disorders organizations and charities

There are a number of eating disorders organizations whose help and advice can be really useful. They often have staff who have experienced an eating disorder themselves, so can really understand what you are going through. Most run helplines and some offer a range of other services including signposting to counselling organizations and to self-help material and other literature. Joining an organization is a very good way to feel part of a wider group of people struggling with similar issues. See the **Useful resources** section for details of the main eating disorders charities.

Support groups

Support groups exist worldwide and can be a very good source of support and help towards recovery for both sufferers and carers. Support groups are usually run by someone who has experienced an eating disorder themselves and has gone on to recover so they have relevant, hands-on experience along with many skills to impart, as well as visible hope for recovery.

Counselling and other therapies

Counselling is all about giving you some time and space to talk through how you are feeling, and offers a really valuable opportunity to sort out your thoughts and to have someone you can talk to without having to worry what they think about you. You may be referred by your doctor or you can approach a counsellor yourself. Your doctor and the eating disorder organizations listed in the Useful Resources section will be able to direct you to private counsellors in your area.

Specialist services

Your doctor will be able to talk to you about specialist services such as regular counselling and nutritional advice. If needs be, your doctor will refer you to a specialist for treatment. Services will vary according to where you live; in the UK, for example, you may be referred to the Eating Disorder Service, which offers treatment for either adults or children and adolescents, depending on your age.

Hospital and inpatient unit

If someone's physical or mental health deteriorates to a point of real concern, then inpatient care might well be suggested, at either a hospital with an eating disorders unit or at a separate unit. Although this can be a very hard stage for sufferers and their families to come to terms with initially, it can often be a turning point for sufferers in their decision to accept and access help. On hand are nurses trained in mental health, dieticians, psychiatrists, and psychologists, many of whom have specialist knowledge.

Note that if you or someone you are supporting experiences an emergency admission for medical care (say after a collapse or medical emergency), it may well be that you or they are initially admitted to a general medical ward rather than one that specializes in eating disorders. While this is often necessary to stabilize the person (and for emergency treatment such as rehydration and replacing electrolytes, etc.), it is important that they are moved to a specialist ward as soon as possible. Don't be afraid to ask for this. Emergency medical care, particularly for those who are very low weight, can be extremely traumatic and complex, involving all kinds of ethical and even legal issues. It is something that should be handled by people with good experience and specialist knowledge of eating disorders.

Family and friends

We'll look at the role of other people who can support you in recovery in later chapters, but we can't leave out friends and family members when we're thinking about where you can find support. As they are the ones who care about you the most, they will be the ones who want to find as much help for you as they can. Sometimes of course they may appear to be trying too hard. Give them a chance – if they feel overbearing it is only because they care. Remember also that your own perception of how well or unwell you are might not be that reliable. Your friends and family can be a direct source of both emotional and practical help (after all, who is going to drive you to all those appointments?), as well as being able to find you other forms of support. They can also help you with difficult decisions or the many seemingly daunting steps involved in seeking treatment.

What if it all goes horribly wrong?

We can't leave this chapter without considering everyone's worst fear: what if you seek help and the response you get is everything you have dreaded? While this is unusual, some people do find that those they have reached out to are not as understanding as they think. Some people may say or do things that they think are helpful, but actually are hurtful. Some may just not take things seriously. If this happens to you then do not panic or lose all your resolve.

These reactions usually have their roots in ignorance – so don't give up.

If your doctor is not very helpful, remember that not all have the same knowledge and experience of eating disorders. In the UK, guidelines for the treatment of eating disorders were published in 2004 and these guidelines may help you assess the quality of the care you're receiving. They are based on research findings from all over the world and offer an indication of what is best practice and can be a useful standard. (You can find details of how to get hold of these NICE guidelines in the **Useful resources** section, p. 90.) If you are experiencing any difficulties with your doctor, talk to him or her and explain the problem or how you feel. There may be another doctor in the practice who has more experience of or interest in emotional health issues and you can ask to see them. If you wish, you can even ask to move to another surgery altogether.

Sometimes people have unfortunate experiences of other therapists or professionals offering them support. Again this usually stems from someone who does not have sufficient understanding or expertise in eating disorders. If you are looking for a private therapist or counsellor, don't be afraid to ask if they have experience of working with eating disorders or if they have done any specialist training. Many eating disorders charities and support groups will also be able to give you lists of specialist therapists in your area, so if in doubt, speak to them first.

Whoever you see for treatment, remember their role is to help you to work towards recovery – and that means that they need to have the same idea and concept of recovery as you do. Talk to them about what their aims for you are and make sure you are both working towards the same thing. Most therapists offer an initial appointment just to meet and talk about what their help would involve, so do use this and don't be afraid to ask questions – even take along any notes or thoughts you have.

The most important thing in any treatment is that you find someone you can trust and work with – although it takes time to build up this trust. If you are experiencing treatment that makes you uncomfortable or which you feel is not helping, always discuss this with the therapist – or if you feel you can't, talk to your doctor.

7

The role of other people in recovery

Many people who develop eating disorders are life's "copers" – they tend to be very independent and get on with things on their own. Accepting help and support from other people often doesn't come naturally and might even feel like an admission of some kind of failure.

What people say…
I find it hard to rely on other people. I try not to bother other people and mostly I keep myself to myself. I support lots of other people and I don't want them thinking that they need to be looking after me. But treatment has helped me to realize that my eating disorder developed because it was too much to cope on my own all the time. I know I am going to have to get over this and let people help me – one step at a time.
   Suzanne

Letting others support you

Letting others help you in order to tackle and eventually overcome your eating disorder is probably the first step you will take on the path to recovery. Of course, building up relationships with medical or therapeutic professionals is invaluable, but so too is having a network of support from others when the weekly or fortnightly sessions with professionals are over. In fact it's often those times in between sessions – when you are trying to put into practice the advice from the professionals working with you – that people find they need support the most. Loneliness, isolation, low mood and depression and, issues with self-worth are common features of an eating disorder and you may well be someone who struggles to think of yourself in a good light or to remain motivated and on course. Having someone to remind you of your good qualities, someone who likes you and loves you despite your eating problems, and who reminds you that you can get through this and recover, is invaluable.

Over to you: Who could you call on?

The first step in getting support from other people is to know who to ask. Think about the people in your life at the moment who might be able to help you. They might be people who could answer your questions or who would give you space to talk – perhaps people who are older than you such as relatives, youth leaders, teachers, etc. Or they might be people more "on your level" – people you would spend time with and whose company you enjoy. You might think that right now you couldn't ask some of them for support, but don't let that rule them out. Instead write a list of possible people and try to avoid ruling them out before you have even written them down!

Next, look over your list and choose a few people whom you know you can really rely on. Can you do anything to enable them to support you? Maybe you need to tell them what is going on and admit that you have a problem you are struggling to overcome? Could you arrange to meet somewhere so you have space to talk? You might want to try to arrange a regular get-together with someone, so that you know you have predictable space where you can talk things through. Remember, you're not looking for a bunch of amateur therapists! These people are friends – some of them may provide more than others in the way of advice, but the main thing is connecting with them and sharing something of yourself and your journey.

When you have decided on a few people, write down their names and then think about what actions you need to take in order to start to build on this supportive relationship. Do you need to arrange a coffee with them? Or perhaps write them an email? Note down anything that you plan to do in order to develop this friendship – this is the first step in your plan to start to build on your support networks.

For those caring – what can you do?

There's one common question that those supporting sufferers as they work towards recovery often ask and it's this: "But what can I *do*?" Watching an eating disorder from the outside is very hard and can bring up all kinds of emotions like despair, anxiety, frustration, and even anger that this person whom you love is going through something so hard and cannot see themselves the way you see them.

Don't forget how important simple practical support can be. This might involve driving to appointments, collecting prescriptions, helping with shopping (which can be a long and difficult task during early recovery in particular), being with them during mealtimes or challenging times, or when accomplishing goals like eating out. You can also help the person you are supporting to keep up a social life that does not revolve around the eating disorder, because they may have become quite isolated.

Who are you?

Perhaps the most important thing to ask yourself when caring for someone else is what your role is and your relationship to the sufferer. Who you are in relation to them makes a big difference in how you will be able to support them. Think about your role and the practical implications it has. Sometimes the people who might seem to be in the perfect position to help someone are actually too close and find it very difficult to bring up the subject of what is going on. Particularly very close relationships – for example if it is your partner or spouse who is struggling – can very easily become dominated by the eating disorder, and you may want to try to keep your relationship separate from what is going on. Don't be afraid to admit the natural limits to your role – whatever it is – and think about who else might be in a good place to offer support in a way that is different from yours.

I am really worried about my friend. Should I say anything?

This can be a tricky position to be in and how much you are able to do will depend on how close you are to the sufferer. You may even have guessed that there is a problem rather than being told. If this is the case then respect their privacy and resist the temptation to confront them. If you do they will most likely react defensively and with fear, and you will have lost the opportunity to help.

Instead support them by being a friend. Meet up with them and enjoy shared interests. Where you can, talk to them about their life and how they are feeling *generally*. Give them time and space so that if they want to, they can share more of what they are feeling.

Of course, if you are very concerned, and if you feel that it is possible no one else knows, you may have to talk to them about their eating disorder, but be very gentle and non-confrontational. You might want to try writing them a letter or card rather than talking face to face, and then invite them to talk to you if they want to. Help them to take steps such as seeing their doctor, and be there for them throughout treatment – whatever the outcome. Beware of well-meaning offers that you cannot keep up, like inviting them to live with you or to eat every meal with you. Remember that recovery is a long road and might involve many ups and downs – be prepared to see it through with them.

Above all, though, just be a friend. For someone with an eating disorder, having someone who will listen without trying to advise or "fix" them is often one of the most important means of support.

What people say...

I felt that I was a burden, just a sick person needing weekly appointments and follow-ups... Therefore all my time was spent with doctors who were understandably talking about my eating in trying to help me recover, but who talked incessantly about "my condition" and about food. I felt I was talked at and sometimes I came away very angry. At home my mum was nagging me constantly about food. It was so good to be able to let it all out to my friend. She just listened. She didn't know much about eating disorders (and that was probably just as well), but she was interested in me and asked me things about it and how I felt. Mostly though we talked about normal things like what was happening in our favourite soaps and about her job. That made me feel normal and proved that she still liked me despite my eating disorder.

Erin

8

Getting back in control

For most sufferers the worst thing about their eating disorder is feeling out of control – in relation to eating, their weight or other symptoms such as purging – and any physical side effects. All of these are related to the chaotic patterns which sufferers get caught up in – that diet–binge–purge cycle (see Chapter 2). This chapter offers some simple guidelines for how to start to break out of these cycles. If you work through these steps alongside getting some other expert help, you can start to regain some control over your eating, reduce purging and hopefully therefore make life easier with people, especially those who are worrying about you.

If you have an eating disorder, you just need to sort your eating out and then everything will be fine.
This is often what you imagine people are thinking when you are the one stuck in the midst of an eating disorder.

One sufferer remembers someone saying, "I wish we could just put two stone on you and then everything would be OK." They meant well – she was experiencing a lot of stress and pressure because her weight was so low – but to her it felt as if all they cared about was what she weighed. This chapter isn't here because your eating and purging are all that you need to get sorted out. But in simple everyday terms, issues like chaotic eating, bingeing, and purging are what can make each day feel so dreadful. Bringing back a level of control to these things will not solve all your problems, but it is a good place to start.

Moving back towards "normal" eating

The first step in overcoming the vicious cycle of eating disorders is perhaps the hardest one. This is to stop the diet phase and reintroduce "normal" eating. It is hard because it involves letting go of the hope you had, that restricting your eating would solve the other problems in your life. This is the reason we spent so much time in Chapters 3 and 4 looking at what you wanted for your future. You need to know very firmly why you do not want to continue with the eating disorder. Secondly, you need to understand how your eating pattern is keeping you trapped in this horrid unhelpful cycle.

Over to you: Why do you want to let go of your eating disorder?

The process of recovering from an eating disorder is not easy – and at times everyone finds the old urges hard to fight. In those moments you need to remember exactly why you want to recover – and why you do not want to return to your eating disorder. Take a moment now to list some of the reasons why you do not want to carry on with the eating disorder. You may want to refer back to your lists of the pros and cons of the eating disorder from Chapter 4. Once you have listed the reasons, try to write yourself a quick note explaining why you have decided to leave the eating disorder behind. Some people find it helpful to write it almost as a letter, saying goodbye to their eating disorder and explaining why they have to let it go. You may prefer to do this on a separate sheet of paper.

Once you have done this, keep it in a safe place. You may find in those tough moments that you need to return and re-read it – and remind yourself of why you are working so hard to move on.

Returning to normal eating is not something that you will be able to do overnight. There are three important stages to work through.

Stage 1: What on earth is normal?

Most people who have suffered with an eating disorder admit to forgetting what normal eating means. Particularly if you have been restricting your eating for a long time, you may well have totally lost touch with what a normal amount of food is. Research shows that a lot of eating disorder sufferers underestimate how much it is normal to eat and panic unnecessarily when they start to increase their meal size.

Over to you: Getting an idea of what normal eating is

This will require you to enlist the help of a few friends or family members. Choose people who you know have a healthy attitude towards food and their weight. Go for people who are the most "normal" eaters you know! Ask them if they will keep a food diary for you over a normal three-day period. They should note down everything they eat and when they eat it. So, meals would go down there, but also snacks, teas and coffees, maybe a chocolate or biscuit with the teas and coffees – everything! They might find this quite hard because they probably don't think about what they eat that much – but it will be really helpful for you.

Once you have three people's food diaries, sit down and have a read through them. Is there anything that surprised you? Can you now make some notes about what normal eating is and is not?

Stage 2: Starting to improve eating patterns

This is where the help of a good friend or even a professional such as the practice nurse or a nutritionist or dietician can really be valuable. You need to work upwards from what you currently eat and move towards a normal diet. Here are two things to aim at:

- First, aim to move towards eating three proper meals each day. It might take you a while to get here if what you currently eat (or aim to eat) is a lot less. Take it in little steps – for example, if you don't eat any real meals, think about which is the least scary meal and try to work towards making sure you manage to eat at least that meal each day. So, if breakfast is least scary, aim to eat a breakfast each day. Then gradually improve what you eat at that meal until it meets what you might call a "normal" breakfast level. You'll need some help with this, and that's where someone else's opinion comes in. Once you feel comfortable with eating that meal, move on to try to introduce the next least scary – and so on.

- If you are used to eating more or struggling with binge eating, it's really important that you put back into place a reasonable eating pattern as soon as possible. Now you might worry that all this eating will trigger your urge to binge, and we'll be honest – at first you might find it hard. But the urge to binge is maintained by the fact that your body is not getting enough regular and predictable meals. Similar urges have been found in people who were deliberately fed starvation diets as part of research decades ago. If you keep going and eat regularly and healthily, the urges will subside.

What IS normal eating?

It's slightly difficult to define what normal eating is, because everyone is different – but here are some things *it usually includes*. What do you think? Is there anything you would add?

Normal eating is...
- ✓ Choosing your food by what you fancy, albeit while also trying to eat reasonably healthily.
- ✓ Sometimes aiming to include certain things in your diet, e.g. five fruit and veg.
- ✓ Not forbidding anything, although some things are eaten much less often than others.
- ✓ Eating at least three meals a day, plus snacks.
- ✓ Responding to hunger by eating.
- ✓ Sometimes eating too much, sometimes too little – and letting it balance out naturally.
- ✓ Sometimes eating in response to boredom, or to certain emotions.
- ✓ Enjoying food at social occasions – eating out or with friends from time to time.

It doesn't include...

x   Counting calories, fat grams, etc. or reading the back of the packet before you can eat something.

x   Avoiding or cutting out certain food groups altogether.

x   Feeling guilty and worrying about what you are eating or have eaten.

x   Using food to try to cope with how you are feeling.

x   Compensating for having eaten by then going without.

x   Having to prepare everything yourself.

x   Eating only in secret or when you are on your own.

If you are finding the urge to binge very powerful, get someone to supervise mealtimes and help control what you eat. Or you can plan to go out and do something after each meal, such as take a walk or go to visit a friend. Getting out of the house, or wherever your binges usually take place, is often very helpful and the urge usually fades as a result. Of course, your binge/diet cycle is also controlled by how you feel, so do be aware of your emotions. Hopefully you will be getting extra help or support for this side of your eating disorder, but you might want to note down how you were feeling if you do slip up and have a binge. Look for patterns and then try to think of how you can address the emotion that triggered the binge instead of giving in and eating.

One more thing – if you do slip up and binge, don't fall into the trap of immediately condemning yourself. It's so easy to think, "Well that's it, what a waste of space. I've totally blown it now and I'll never get over this." Everyone recovering from an eating disorder has times when they slip up – it's a normal part of recovery. The key to how long this goes on for is how you react to those moments. Do you slip into despair and self-hatred, or do you use the opportunity to understand better what triggered it, so that you can make it less likely to happen next time?

Stage 3: Adding variety
The next thing to work towards to improve your diet is to increase the variety of what you eat. Most people with eating disorders end up eating quite a narrow diet – and that monotony can contribute towards urges and cravings.

Over to you: Rating your forbidden foods!

Before you start introducing foods back into your diet, make a list of the foods you currently avoid, and give each a score on a scale of 0 to 10, where 0 means it is totally safe (actually that probably means you already include it in your diet!) and 10 means it is utterly terrifying.

When you start adding foods back into your diet, start with the ones which have the lowest scores. How quickly you aim to reintroduce them is up to you. You might want to add all the foods with a score of 1 in the first week, for example, then when you feel ready, reintroduce all foods which score 2, and so on. Or you might want to choose one food at a time to reintroduce. If your diet has become very limited, as it might have if you have been suffering with anorexia, you may well need some help with this. In particular, if your weight is very low and improving your diet is crucial, help will be important. Ask your doctor if a dietician or anyone from the practice can see you weekly and help you to improve your diet.

Slow and steady wins the race!

The most common mistake when trying to regain control of eating patterns is to try to do too much too soon. If you have hardly eaten for months, or if your eating has been very out of control, managing to reintroduce one regular planned meal a day might be a huge step. So take this slowly and do it at your own pace and with some good support from friends, family, and professionals around you.

9

What about purging?

As well as looking at how to regain control over your eating there is one other thing people commonly need help with and which deserves specific mention, and that is purging.

What people say...
I've been in recovery for a while now and it's been going pretty well. I haven't binged in a while and I am eating much better. But I am struggling terribly with the desire to purge. Every time I eat I find myself thinking about going and making myself sick, and I have to confess I still take laxatives every day. Without them I feel really full and uncomfortable and I just don't manage to eat as well. What can I do to break this cycle of purging?

 Steven, recovering from bulimia

Mythbuster

Purging is a safe way of controlling your weight.
This is NOT true! Almost all methods used hold very real risks which can be extremely serious (see Chapter 3). Many people have suffered serious consequences or even death because of the unintended effects of what they were doing; accidents or injuries resulting from their purging; or taking tablets or medication without realizing what they really were or what they really did.

Purging – in whatever form it takes – is increasingly common. An eating disorder can fill you with panic, and in the midst of that there is the risk that you will turn to anything in the desperate hope that it will stop you putting on weight, without realizing the risks you may be taking.

The ultimate deception
Purging really is a wolf in sheep's clothing. It sets itself up as something it is not. Sufferers purge because they believe it helps. Without it they feel they would be huge, enormous, and obese. But studies show that sufferers really do not gain weight because they have usually not eaten as much as they had feared – their perception of what they should "allow" themselves to eat has become very distorted by their illness.

Perhaps the most sinister thing about purging, however, is that it actually makes things *worse*. If you are caught up in cycles of binge eating, once you believe there is something you can do *after eating* which might stop you from putting weight on, control breaks down still further, and you eat more and more. For some people binges develop over time and become more serious and more frequent. Sufferers report a sense of urgency and panic, and often report not even having properly tasted the food. Some will plan for binges, buying food specifically for it, whereas others might find their loss of control means they eat food that is not theirs or eat food that they would never usually consider, such as food that is not cooked or still frozen.

In that sense, purging can become immensely psychologically addictive. It becomes part of the cycles of fear and panic. Many people find that their purging develops or escalates. Someone who starts just taking a dose of laxatives after a binge eventually finds themselves swallowing handfuls of tablets every day. Occasionally making yourself sick leads to feeling guilty if you let yourself keep *anything* down. And all the time, while the fear and dread of gaining weight grows, binge eating also gets worse.

There *is* a way to stop!
So what can you do to break free from the guilt and fear that keeps you purging, and how should you get started?

1 Talk to your doctor
This is particularly important if you have been taking laxatives over a long period of time or in large quantities. If your body has got used to the impact they have had over this long period of time, then stopping them abruptly might cause a lot of discomfort – and it's therefore best to have your doctor's advice and support as you gradually reduce the quantity you take. Whatever the method of

purging, it is good to talk things through with your doctor. He or she will be able to reassure you about any health consequences and will also give you clear and accurate information about any impact that purging might be having on your body.

2 Understand the effect that purging has and the effects it doesn't have

This is really the key to stopping purging. Purging is something that most people start because they are overwhelmed with fear and guilt, and want to stop themselves from gaining weight. They believe that the only thing stopping them from gaining weight is the purging. That belief means that if they ever try not to purge, the fear and guilt comes back twice as strongly as before.

The truth is, purging has much less impact than you might think on how much food is absorbed. Laxatives in particular actually have their impact much further down the digestive system than the place where food absorption takes place. They have their effect either by using bulking agents which absorb water and then expand, meaning that your bowel has more waste to push against, or by irritating the bowel lining so that the waste moves along more quickly.

This means not as much water is taken back up into the body, and more is lost than usual. People often say how they feel "empty" after laxatives have taken their effect – and it may well be that you are losing a lot of something, but it is water, not fat. Water, of course, makes up a massive percentage of your body, so you *will* see a change if you get on the scales – but not because of what you think. Plus, water is really important to your body and the next time you drink or eat something with water in it you'll find the "weight" going straight back on.

So not only did the laxatives deceive you and make you think you lost weight when you didn't really, they then make you really paranoid another day because it feels as if out of nowhere you put loads of weight back on! Even *normal* changes in hydration can result in as much as one kilogram of weight difference in twenty-four hours (that's a couple of pounds) – so imagine how much chaos it can cause if you are losing, and then regaining, more water than usual. In addition, dehydration makes you feel low and sluggish and can add to the urge to binge – so it really does strengthen the vicious cycles you are caught up in.

Even things like making yourself sick or exercising a lot are not as powerful as you might think. When you make yourself sick, again what most people don't realize is how much digestive fluid (and more water) they are losing rather than actual food. As anyone will know if they have seen a child throw up, it always looks much more than it is. Most people make themselves sick bring up a lot less food than they think. Meanwhile, exercise is great for keeping healthy, but as a method of working off food it is pretty hard work! Even strenuous exercise like running or cycling burns only about 500 calories in an hour – and you'll find you can eat that many calories much more quickly than you can burn them off. Believing that this works makes bingeing worse (see Chapter 2). In addition, excessive exercise might not be as effective as you think, and eventually can cause danger to your heart and affect the stability of your health if you are at a very low weight.

As well as accepting the truth about what purging

doesn't do, talk to your doctor about any negative side effects. You need to know the truth about any risks you are taking. Then only you can decide whether it is really worth it?

3 Start to cut down

Exactly how you do this is something you and your doctor will want to decide. Once you realize the negative impact purging is really having, you may find that you want to give it up straight away. Sometimes there are good medical reasons not to stop abruptly (see above), so do check with your doctor. If you want or need to cut down more gradually, think about how you could do this – perhaps reducing how often you purge or taking fewer laxatives, exercising for a shorter time or at a lower intensity. Share your plans with someone else and ask for their help. Most of all, though, remember *why* you want to cut down. Ultimately stopping purging is part of breaking free of that diet–binge–purge cycle. Very few people will be able to stop bingeing while still allowing themselves to keep purging. So take a risk, pluck up the courage, and break the cycle.

10

Recovery – so much can change...

We could have put so many people's experiences of recovery here but there isn't room. Here's just one. Remember – look forward and do not be overwhelmed by how far away your future seems.

What people say...
At the age of twenty-eight, having recovered from anorexia is one of my biggest achievements to date. I have read so many stories of recovery, and always thought they were lying, but actually you can beat an eating disorder... I have.

Recovery for me started seven years ago in 2002 when I was hospitalized. To set the scene, it was four months before my twenty-first birthday; I weighed thirty-two kilograms, had a BMI of eleven, and had two weeks to live. I fought as much as I could, but one morning two nurses came into my room, held my head back, and as I swallowed they put a tube up my nose and into my stomach. As it turned out, this was probably the best thing that ever happened to me.

I was in hospital for two months, and during that time I got to know staff really well. One nurse gave me perhaps the best piece of advice I have ever been given. He said that I could beat this if I kept it academic. He was right – I was a grade A student. So, I sat all day in hospital researching in books, and devising my own treatment plan with the help of my medical team.

Recovery is not easy, but it is achievable if you prepare yourself for hard work. It's taken me seven years, and I have only just fully recovered. It's always going to be hard but there are ways of coping, and in my mind it's being prepared and knowledgeable. Know what you are in for, and you can beat it. You need your friends and family more than anything else, and luckily for me, mine were 100 per cent supportive at all times. I could tell them anything. These are your main tools, and will be for a long time. They love you.

Keeping it academic worked really well for me, especially for the first few months. I was still in denial until my brain had enough energy to function. Weight is just numbers, food intake is just another task in your day. It can hold no emotion. With every pound you gain, you have to realize what a great event it is. You are achieving.

You have to be honest with yourself and with others. Don't expect too much of yourself, or a miracle. You would be setting yourself up to fail. I didn't tell a lot of people either, even though at my worst it was obvious. Let's face it, sufferers deserve an Oscar for the acting performance they put on. Everything's fine, everything's wonderful. Well no it isn't actually. A lot of people I have met over the past few years don't even know I had anorexia. I think my recovery would have come on a lot quicker if I had been honest with people.

At some points you think you are recovered, because you are slightly better, or because you don't look anorexic any more. You won't realize it can get even better until it actually does. Once you get through the scary and distressing parts of recovery, it actually becomes fun. I know this seems like another lie, but it's true. Developing a sense of self after years of being completely detached from life is exciting. Throughout recovery you are essentially like a cardboard cut-out of yourself; you're present, but it's not you. Even when you want to be emotionally involved, you can't. Things just happen to you rather than involve you.

Seven years on from being tube-fed, my outlook is good. I have different priorities in life now and know that there are more important things in life than what size you are. I am just like any other 28-year-old and want the same things in life. I have never been happier than I am now.

Laura

For the family

If someone in your family is fighting an eating disorder, the strain and emotions affect everyone. Here are some tips for all the family.

For parents
This is perhaps the most challenging position to be in. In some ways you might think that parents are in the ideal place to support a sufferer. The truth is that they are often in a terribly difficult position, torn between being the friend and emotional support, but also expected to "enforce" homework tasks set by therapists, and to supervise diet and mealtimes, often with little or no help from professionals.

The uncomfortable reality is that most parents experience aggressive, even violent behaviour from their child – whatever their age. You may be the person your child feels most comfortable with and this means you are likely to be the one against whom they vent most of their difficult and scariest feelings. Remember that these are emotions triggered by the illness spilling over. They are rarely personal. Sometimes the best thing to do is to withdraw; other times it may be that these are feelings that your child needs to express. However, these emotions should not be an excuse or justification for unacceptable behaviour, so do draw limits. Try to find times when things are calmer to talk things over with your child and agree how you will both cope in those moments when things get fraught. Avoid confrontation where you can. If you feel that professionals are expecting you to be the "bad guy", don't just go along with it – talk to them about it.

Do not try to support your child without any support yourself. Seeking and accepting help from others will make you much more able to support your child well, and will also teach them a valuable lesson – that it is OK to need other people. For more details of where you can get support and advice specifically for parents, see the Resources section.

How parents can help a child with an eating disorder – some simple DOs and DON'Ts!

✓ DO try not to focus on the food and eating but on how your child is feeling and coping generally with life.

✓ DO try to understand eating disorders and get some information, support and advice from one of the organizations listed.

✓ DO help your child to seek professional help as early as possible and be a part of the process.

✓ DO view the eating disorder separately from your child.

✓ DO be firm with the eating disorder, but offer unconditional love and support to your child.

x   DON'T ignore the signs of eating distress. Encourage your child to talk. Listen to them.

x   DON'T be angry or use emotional blackmail.

x   DON'T despair or give up. Get some support yourself – if you can carry hope for your child, you will help them too believe that one day they can get through this.

Mythbuster

You can't help your child unless they want to help themselves.

There is an element of truth in this, but it doesn't mean that there is nothing you can say or do if they do not appear to want help. You may need to get medical help for your child if they are at risk physically. Children who are growing can become physically ill very quickly and your intervention can be vital. Although the key to recovery is helping people to really want recovery *themselves,* your support may be crucial in getting them to admit that something is wrong and then doing something about it. If the only reason they are contemplating change is because you are nagging them, any attempts at recovery will be futile. If they do not want help or do not think there is a problem, you might want to read the first two chapters of this book with them. Remember that an eating disorder means they risk not thinking about it until it is too late and they are already somewhere they didn't intend to be.

A special note about adult children living away from home

It is particularly hard for parents to provide help and encouragement for a sufferer if they are living away from home. Parents worry about their child however old they are and can become very distressed and anxious if they consider their child's health to be at risk and are excluded from the facts and from helping them. Sometimes the emotion makes the relationship strained and makes it more difficult for the sufferer to "open up", but it also gives the eating disorder the opportunity to grow undisturbed. If your "child" is an adult, don't stand by while they deteriorate, but do remember that someone else may be in a better position than you to help.

For dads...

Being the dad or step-dad of someone with an eating disorder presents particular challenges – whether you are a single dad managing your child's eating disorder alone, or part of a partnership. Fathers often describe their reaction to the eating disorder as one of incredulity mixed with anger.

What people say...

I could see the problem and I just wanted to fix it. I know my attempts came out all wrong with quite a lot of aggression and I was a bit of a rhino really, but I saw myself as head of the family with a child who was slipping into danger and yet who wouldn't (or couldn't as I appreciate now) listen to me.
  Phil

Fathers are often trying to keep the home going as normal and trying to go to work as usual, however difficult it is to keep their mind on the job.

What people say...

My career and our livelihood were in danger. I wasn't able to concentrate and give my job my usual commitment when our son was ill. I also had to take a lot of time out for his appointments and family therapy sessions. My wife needed a lot of extra support from me too, so too my other kids, which put considerable strain on me. I admit to dreading coming home and staying late at the office because the atmosphere was so fraught at home. In all honesty I wanted to avoid facing mealtimes with my son and a home life which was out of control.

Richard

If you are a dad trying to cope with an eating disorder, then do accept that you will probably react in a very different way to your partner. Find somewhere you can take these emotions and express them, so that you are more likely to be able to hold it together when you are at home. Your role may well be crucial – research suggests that the way dads respond to therapy and treatment for eating disorders can be very important. However, talking and approaches such as family therapy may be very alien to you and rather difficult at first. Be realistic about what you can and cannot do and don't be afraid to admit your limitations.

Sometimes the relationship between dads and professionals can be difficult. Some dads have reported that they felt people were suspicious of them or felt that their behaviour or responses were being monitored. Others have found that when they reacted with anger, they were suspected of being abusive or overly aggressive. Remember that anxiety, fear or even the urge to cry can come out as anger and aggression. Try not to feel paranoid, but it is essential that you stay controlled.

What about husbands/wives/partners?

Being in this close a relationship with someone suffering is very hard. You may be struggling with some difficult feelings surrounding their eating disorder – particularly if they have kept it a secret from you for a long time. You need to acknowledge those feelings or the likelihood is that they will spill out as you try to care for your partner. Remember also that your relationship is one that ideally is based on equal roles. You do not want to become a parent to them and they are unlikely to want this either.

One common problem is the impact that an eating disorder can have on someone's ability to show or accept love and affection. You may find that your partner struggles with any physical form of affection or becomes very anxious about what you think of their body or weight. Try to avoid getting involved in discussions about their weight. Instead provide gentle reassurance and help them to divert their thinking to something else.

Meanwhile there will be times when all the anxiety and strain is expressed as outright anger or hostility – often towards you. Many partners describe the unpredictability of living with someone who alternates between needing them so much and then seeming frustrated and angry with them. Remember that some of this comes from the eating disorder and from the impact that things like low blood sugar levels can have on their moods. Try to give them space and be there when they need you, but do remember that there are some kinds of behaviour that are simply not acceptable. Be kind but firm if they are treating you unreasonably, and make sure you get good advice and support. You may wish to seek some joint counselling or support to help both of you cope with the impact that working through the eating disorder can have on your relationship.

Siblings

Siblings often feel forgotten about when an eating disorder occurs at home. Suddenly a lot of attention can be focused on the person suffering, and siblings may feel left out or invisible. At the same time siblings have to cope with living in a situation which has suddenly become very stressful. They too experience the arguments, the unbearably tense family meals, and the anxiety over what will happen next.

If your brother or sister has an eating disorder, remember that it is OK for you to find the situation hard as well. It may be difficult for you to find time and space which is not dominated by the eating disorder, so see if you can arrange to spend time with friends or with other family members which is just for *you*. A regular time with your mum or dad on your own can give you space to chat and to make sure there is time for you.

Siblings often struggle with feeling guilty or with worrying if something they have said or done caused the eating disorder. Remember that an eating disorder is very complicated. You will not have caused it! All siblings argue sometimes, and during those arguments most people say things they later regret. If there are genuinely things you wish you had not said, then why not write a letter, email or card and let your brother or sister know. Don't be afraid to tell them that you love them. If you can find time to spend with them without the eating disorder being at the front of everyone's mind, this will be really helpful – so if there are things you used to do together, try to keep doing them.

Finally, it's not unusual for siblings to struggle with thoughts and feelings about their own eating or weight. With so much focus and discussion on these things you might find yourself thinking about them in a way you wouldn't usually. Make sure you find a channel to talk about these things. It may be that someone from school or somewhere else – a teacher, counsellor or youth worker – can meet up with you from time to time so that you have some space to share your thoughts. Remember that you do still have your own needs – don't feel guilty for these or try to suppress them.

What people say...

I felt frightened and helpless – a bit of a spare part really. I also felt angry at the situation and with everyone. The advice and support we received helped me understand my feelings and made me realize that I did have a part to play in my sister's recovery and that together we could all get her through.

Holly

Whatever your role in the family, remember that there are places you can get support and advice that is relevant to your particular situation. See the **Useful resources** section for some contact details and sources of support.

Please be encouraged that getting that advice and support early on provides the best possible basis for helping someone who is struggling with an eating disorder to achieve recovery and freedom.

Useful resources

Further support

For further help or support, contact one of the organizations in your country:

UK

Anorexia and Bulimia Care (ABC) is one of the two national UK eating disorder organizations. It has a Christian foundation and supports all who suffer because of eating disorders. It provides information, literature, advice, and support, as well as a unique befriending service, matching someone struggling with an eating disorder to someone who has had experience of recovery, in order to support and encourage them. ABC has dedicated telephone and email helplines; one for sufferers and one for parents and all those concerned.

Website: www.anorexiabulimiacare.co.uk
"tbh" blog site for young people: www.tobehonest.org.uk
Sufferer Support Line: 01934 710 679
Email: sufferersupport@anorexiabulimiacare.co.uk
Parent Support Line: 01934 710 645
Email: ache@anorexiabulimiacare.co.uk

BEAT (previously the Eating Disorders Association) is the largest organization in the UK working with eating disorders. BEAT offers information and help, as well as running support groups and providing various resources.

Website: www.b-eat.co.uk

Tel: 0845 634 1414

Email: help@b-eat.co.uk

Helpline for young people: 0845 634 7650 (text on 07786 201 820) or email help@b-eat.co.uk or fyp@b-eat.co.uk

USA

National Eating Disorders Association (NEDA) is dedicated to providing education, resources and support to those affected by eating disorders – whether you are an individual living with an eating disorder, a family member or friend looking to offer support to a loved one, or a treatment professional looking to help others.

Website: www.nationaleatingdisorders.org

Binge Eating Disorders Association (BEDA). Binge eating disorder is the most common eating disorder in the USA. BEDA is committed to helping those who suffer from binge eating disorder conquer their disorder.

Website: www.bedaonline.com

Australia

Butterfly Foundation provides support for Australians who suffer from eating disorders and negative body image issues, and for their carers.

Website: www.thebutterflyfoundation.org.au

Eating Disorders Foundation of Victoria Inc aims to provide sufferers of eating disorders and their families and friends with up-to-date information about the various eating disorders and about services and resources in Victoria to assist recovery.
Website: www.eatingdisorders.org.au

New Zealand

Eating Disorders Association of NZ (EDANZ) offers help to parents and carers. EDANZ was established by parents of people with eating disorders in New Zealand.
Website: www.ed.org.nz

Eating Difficulties Education Network (EDEN) is a non-profit community agency based in Auckland, New Zealand. Their purpose is to promote body trust and satisfaction, size acceptance, and diversity on an individual and societal level.
Website: www.eden.org.nz

Recommended books

If you have found this book helpful and want to read more, there is a more detailed guide covering all the basic information you need to know about eating disorders and how to work towards recovery: *Eating Disorders – The Path to Recovery* is written by Dr Kate Middleton (published by Lion Hudson, ISBN 978 0 7459 5278 9) and is aimed at both sufferers and carers. As well as helping people to understand how eating disorders develop, it has a particular focus on recovery and includes the real-life experiences of current and recovering sufferers all at different stages on their own road to recovery.

There are also some good self-help books available that take you through a series of exercises, based on Cognitive Behavioural Therapy (CBT), designed to help people work towards recovery. *Bulimia Nervosa and Binge-Eating – A Guide to Recovery* (by Peter J. Cooper, published by Constable & Robinson Ltd, ISBN 1-85487-171-4) looks at the cycles of behaviour involved in binge eating and purging and gives a step-by-step programme to work on breaking out of these patterns. *Overcoming Anorexia Nervosa – A self-help guide using cognitive behavioural techniques* (by Chris Freeman, published by Constable & Robinson Ltd, ISBN 1-85487-969-3) looks at the issues more specifically related to anorexia, as well as some of the underlying issues which can be related to the illness.

National Institute for Health and Clinical Excellence (NICE)

The National Institute for Clinical Excellence (NICE) is a group working within the UK health system to produce guidelines for the treatment of all kinds of health issues. Working from research findings, they recommend best practice for treatment. Versions are published for medical professionals, patients, and their families.

THE NICE eating disorder guidelines were published in 2004 and make recommendations for the identification, treatment and management of anorexia, bulimia and other eating disorders (including binge eating disorder) in adults, adolescents and children from eight-years-old.

NICE guidelines on eating disorders – information for the pubic (including patients and their carers): http://guidance.nice.org.uk/CG9/PublicInfo/pdf/English

NICE guidelines on eating disorders – quick reference guide:

http://guidance.nice.org.uk/CG9/QuickRefGuide/pdf/
English

ISBN 978-1-8543-3398-8
www.nice.org.uk

Published by the British Psychological Society,
St Andrews House,
48 Princess Road East,
Leicester
LE1 7DR.
www.bps.org.uk and the Royal College of
Psychiatrists, 17 Belgrave Square, London SW1X 8PG,
www.rcpsych.ac.uk.
Distributed in North America by Balogh International Inc.

Also currently available in the "First Steps" series:

First Steps out of Anxiety
Dr Kate Middleton

First Steps out of Depression
Sue Atkinson

First Steps out of Problem Drinking
John McMahon

Forthcoming in 2011:

First Steps out of Gambling
Lisa Mills and Joanna Hughes

First Steps through Bereavement
Sue Mayfield